THE GIRL IN THE DOG-TOOTH COAT

Zelda Chappel

Thank you!
Zelda Chappel x

BARE FICTION
POETRY

First published in Great Britain by
Bare Fiction
177 Copthorne Road,
Shrewsbury SY3 8NA
www.barefictionmagazine.co.uk

Bare Fiction. Reg. No. 8798494

A CIP catalogue record of this book is available from the British Library.

ISBN: 978-1-910896-00-6
e-book: 978-1-910896-01-3
Kindle: 978-1-910896-02-0

Edited by Robert Harper
Cover image by Jayne Anita Smith

Printed and bound in Great Britain by
Short Run Press, Exeter

For J.S. and E.

Contents

This can be what you want it to be   11

Red sky   12

Flesh   13

Sown   14

Trickster   15

Bathing   16

Skinned   17

Pause   18

Deciphering the sea for my baby   19

Choking   20

Lucky   21

Nature   22

Jolt   23

Removal   24

The muscle feast   25

Moth   26

New year   27

Dating   28

Interlude   29

On finding letters from Aunt F.   30

Promise   31

Old friend   32

Afterwards   33

Renaming   34

A poem in which the sky is a dark envelope   35

The first time we went to bed   36

A poem in which we haven't talked about it yet   37

Lines   38

Search party   39

Dear boy   40

Post-natal   41

Alley   42
Before the birds begin   43
Nightly   44
On leaving me for the American   45
Water   46
Love begins in winter   47
A conversation with the sun   48
Air bubble   49
Exile   50
Another twenty, another stone   51
Dungeness   52
Rooks   53
Winter   54
Dead cert   55
Long rock   56
Creaturely   57
Departing   58
Icon   59
Penny whistle   60
Sound   61
Girl in the dog-tooth coat   62
On not holding on to a bird   63
Sticks   64
Sleep for the insomniac   65
Oblate spheroid   66
Something for nothing   67
Echoes   68
On being lost   69
Numbers   70

ACKNOWLEDGEMENTS   71

I get so close my toes almost touch the salt line, look
for you in yards of empty sea, imagine you stood
on another shore in receipt of all the things I've sent you
drenched in sea air, cool silence
not knowing how well you're placed.

THE GIRL IN THE DOG-TOOTH COAT

This can be what you want it to be

Every now and then we long to leave
our sodium trail on the paving, make
puddles pretend to be skies holding stars.

We've been caught up in the swill,
the dishwater of our slate-hilled predicament,
forgetting what it is to be wild,

nothing but chalk behind glass
and what's worse is we know it all too well.
That distant colt could be us

but we've stopped remembering how it feels
so we ask the birds, begin

to long for their yellowed smiles
their glassed eyes, their oil-soaked skins.

We've been locked in the back streets
of Whitechapel's undertone, instinct
nagging like an echoing bass

wondering how
to unzip our caged bird's chest and find her
tiny heart still beating, how to search
her air-made maps and hold them

let them lead us out of here.

Red sky

In the morning, all we know is the burning dread of it
the warning our Mother gave us nestling in our ears

like a cotton swab, more muffle than substance and sore
unable to be shaken. Keeping watch is simply measured

shades of crimson and rose, a weight that we can assay.
It's tough, but we know the sky—it's our own four walls

no ceiling, a place to calculate tone in silence. Still, we
can't be sure of it. We think of the shepherds alone on

salt-marsh guarding straggles of sheep, the vastness
of longing for water to take what the wind gave us, all

those fears we hold of drowning. We want to hear their
warnings. We've no choice but to slip our skins.

Flesh

It's the ways our tongues get folded, stealing
away my speech. It's open mouths writing

letters, lipped words placed softly in ears
precisely. It's shadows that aren't what they

used to be and my fetish for transcendence.
It's easier. These days it's slipping through

flesh which we know can be done in silence.
It's knowing this is not how you'll have

imagined it. It's not dark except for the door
we're caught behind and my room's heavy

curtains hung drawn, sad, apart for more than
mere sunlight. It's glass making a show

of transparency while I learn the ways to be
opaque. It's shrinking as you fill the space

I leave between my skin and bone. It's waiting
for you to cover me, your skin a fine-spun web.

Sown

Know that I come ready sown and tender
that someone has been here before, decided
to rearrange the furniture. Know that it'll
never be the same, that I am glad for that.
Know that I'm just waiting for the right time
to tell you that when you kiss me, the stitches
unravel from my chest and I am scared
I'll fall open at the wrong page. Know that I
want you to fall right in, that I want you to
learn how to stitch, the right time to unpick.

Trickster

Plain sight is a cloak in itself, so go ahead and deal.
No-one but me sees the way your hand slips under.

Over the fence, Jasper is preening and I am wondering
if I could ever make eyes like emeralds, or if it would matter

if I did. Daylight is a revelation like the apocalypse and I
come ready shattered. The sky always turns eventually.

Comfort is a darkness deep enough to get lost in, the scoop
of the Plough's sweet cradle, the moon's solitary stance.

Bathing

Make a rope swing at the stream we found and I'll be too scared
to navigate it, though I'll like the rhythm of its swoop

how it reminds me of the sea, keeps me listening out for waves.
They are not there. Let me thirst for water between us;

just a few small molecules of separation, that might be enough.
Then force me to work in parchment, blank sheets

I can't unfold. Think my skin is a natural rose and I will tell you
I scrub the inches with a nail brush. Now when I think

of other things, insist I think of you and I'll keep busy making
birds, finding my fingers aren't for wings, still grounded.

Skinned

In the corner, a boy peels my skin with a butter knife
while I watch from the door. He wants it to spiral
like orange peel. It falls like scales instead.

He rarely talks. He chooses instead to stab the air slow
and deliberately. This way he can be sure it registers.
I am meticulous with accounts. I know

the bottom line. He fingers my skin like a typewriter
whose keys are jammed, writes letters that lack
true eloquence. I cannot feel a thing.

Pause

Now that I am airborne, I've become a small full stop. Its perfect
form makes something akin to comfort and I, for one, am grateful.

I could sit this side of the glass or the other and it wouldn't matter.
Transparency means they all pass through and I cannot keep the pace.

In the beginning it was the breaking of things that made most sense
and I grew good at making jigsaws. No-one else minded the gaps.

But you've been determined. Now your hand between my under-skins
gets left there. It helps you know which bits you've touched, which

ones are still to go. I learnt quickly the art of coverage. They'd never
suspect a thing. You've no idea how I could sing a thousand words

and still not be able to speak them. I tell you there's something you
don't understand between the punctuation. I cannot make you learn.

Deciphering the sea for my baby

She is the expanse we feel slipping through our digits
proved in the gritty scratch of displaced sand and shingle
clattering like our neighbour's wind chimes. The clarity
of cold will pull you up sharp, refresh you, draw strong
breath. She's a simple march, a heaving sigh, a scream
between two caves. She talks, just listen—there are stories
she needs to tell, distances that do not end at fingertips.
Get in close and she'll gift you salt without you knowing
cause lips to scale soft until your tongue makes contact
and tastes the alkaline, longs for vinegar. Be warned.
She'll draw you in, stuff your nostrils full of her and sting;
bring tears that are not sad, roll, catch the breaking spray.

Choking

Open me and you'll find my lungs are full of moths
their silvered wings twitching, dying to find the light.

When it's quiet I hear them feasting on the words
that stuck, their dry dust choking them at the source.

These days it's hard to breathe freely; the ways they
steal the air are brazen. I have felt them spinning

casings from the lining, making new bones, beginning.
I wonder constantly at their rebirths, want to know how

to build my own cocoons from the bed sheets, emerge
renewed. They give me no easy answers. Still I'd shun

their wings if I'd been given the chance. I just want
to know how to shape myself in air, that's enough.

Lucky

I was lucky to still be able to find the blue in sky,
the merging greens, the yellow flash of primrose.

I knew earth only through my feet and the backs
of my legs, the glisten of cuckoo spit on the pavement.

You could have talked the world into stopping. It did
for a while. I felt it, the way their backs all turned.

You know I loved the sunset because the blurring
didn't matter. The relief of an ending is always enough.

Nature

You tell me the wind is words
we never said.
          Sometimes I am surprised
by the lack of it.

I have thought about this
                              too much
the place of unseen thought
and unnoticed action

                        where
a twig's snap is temporary
                              and permanent
          all at once and today
that's hard to make sense of.

Your skin
                    could be leaf mulch
in forgotten rain   dark silk
between cold fingers.

          I want to smell you
and know the season
want to know
                    just how ripe we are
how far we've got to go.

Jolt

You leave your words to hang wired, attached
chiming tart from the ceiling rose. From here

the cross-breeze miscounts them, tinned noise
falling out with all time. I'll be a master

of release and her simple, heady expulsion, forget
how my lungs clutch at air with strength

they remember, wait for the time to let go. This
new silence keeps spinning 'til it catches me

whole. Now when you leave, the kitchen clock
loses its power, gets stuck at nine fifteen.

Removal

                        is the wrong word for it
it's surgery   a severance
a replacement of insides with mercury
it takes time   to get it out of your system

it's the debris
of us lying naked in the street
in silence   waiting
for a wind to make it
a tambourine
                        of tin can discord
                                    rattling
                                    clattering
puncturing the sleep-dead night suburbia
as if to say we are still living
                                    alive
            in the sea of could-have-beens.

The muscle feast

Break my shell, reveal the green of weathered copper,
thin mother of pearl in full rainbow split. Show the air
the softness of my flesh but don't forget to let me outline it
for you first. Expose me to the gulls. I cannot wait for sun,
nor the salt of her. Be sure to breathe slow as you do it.
Don't pretend this is not deliberate. Embrace your poise.
It's the middle months that mean the most, their wait.
It's anticipation. The way I've balanced on the cusp in fear
and trust is worse each year, I know. I am more brittle
in this age now sand works hard to do its thing and you
are happy with its scratch. The pulse of dead muscles is
too subtle for your tastes. She'll linger, acrid in the drive
of blood by heart and breath by lung—a slow ratchet click
until I am wound and you are tighter. One day, I'll be fiercer.

Moth

Tell me again how I cannot wear their stains
make wings dust-soft, precise, mere shadow.

I want to be your copper but you see only
earth. I know you'll never change your mind.

In the dark, I still crave the sun. I'm frantic
with my search at times, can't help but pound

the air frustrated. You'll laugh but still I long
to nestle amongst your soft things, lie dormant

build casings in your pockets for weeks, pick
your threads. I imagine your unravelling

like a carousel's spin. I cannot leave my word
so I leave holes for you to stitch, my scent.

I want you to know me. I'll bide my time.

New year

Write to me and tell me how you long for snow, her crisp white
blank, her new beginning. I've watched you, enjoying the poise
of waiting, the rough edge of the cusp of it grinding at our skin
'til we're raw with it. I'm giddy with the drug of it, want you
to be too. In the coming days I'll be looking constantly to sky
for anchorage, unable to predict her moods. I'll learn to absorb
the grey slate wash and pallid days of weakened suns, decipher
punctuation of birds coming home, leaving young. I know you
will be listening as I devour the silence of cold, cold air, trying
to pack it away in my abdomen so I can use it later when time
is hot and frantic. You'll like the way the cold stabs at the heart
of us when we're fighting it. I want you to think of us encrusted
with frost, cracking and spidery across every inch of limb until
we've refracted every piece of light we can. I want you to feel it
when it melts, the sun as it moves into spring, the dead skin
we've slipped and left for ground. I want us to count up all our ends
then bury them with the bulbs, long for the bloom, feel the wait.

Dating

You ask me about my favourite time of year. I can't think
of anything but the yellow flowers on the table—whether
they're real, what they might be called. Tonight before
I came I'd been listening to voices, most of them wrong.
And now, when I try tuning them out, I find myself lost.
I'm out of range and panicked, but you would never tell.
Play the fool and I smile, politely. I'll try rising, find I can't.
They tell me if I let go I could be embraced, encompassed.
I'm not sure that's what I want. I learnt too young the art
of surrender. Now I'm an expert at assessing threat.

Interlude

In the small hours we run ourselves dry of words
and there is nothing left to do but hold each other
awkwardly, side by side on the couch. When I kiss you
all I need to know is that you're kissing me back
that when I slide my hand beneath your t-shirt, you
slip your hand into my hair, cradle the base of my head
while I measure the speed in your heart. And we are
all instinct without thought or care, following blind
as we take turns to remove the layers, your soft hold
making bones dissolve. On the table, whisky glasses
sit spent, ice shrinking slow and shifting.

On finding letters from Aunt F.

The youth of it is startling, crisp as the starched white sheets
she'd fussed over. She longed for the ways they could make
lines in them, for leave and for the heat of it. There was a lot
she left to his own imagination. Knowing him, it could be
vivid. Her trips to the beach every Sunday were all about him
the need to dip her toes in and feel the salt while she learned
the ways the sea could roll like eyes, the feel of shingle
like fingers on her legs. I'm left spellbound by those wistful
days of practice, the work she did to find ways of letting down
her stockings with subtlety, the faces made to mirrors so
she'd know which one to wear in the throes of it, the way
she adjusted the hem of her nightie; she confesses it all.

Promise

I'll make my hair a rose you'll get lost in, mandarin wood
and winter musk carried over to spring. I'll wait for you
to draw the world in through your nostrils,
make them all disappear. As we spin

I'll make red silk and embroider it
to sing against your jeans.

Skin is a short commodity; your lips, my cheek, our fingers
striving to leave themselves in palms. Just in case, I'll print
my eyelashes softly on the cotton of your shoulders.
I wouldn't want you to forget.

You'll be a heron, poised. I know
by the way you stretch

your aim is to wrap me in feathers, despite my fake leather
skins and really, I don't mind. It's the graze of your boot
on my feet when we press, the gentle squeeze
to tell me that we're through.

Old friend

i

In the morning I'll be like the birds that make songs from our poly-cotton bed, take full advantage of the window falling ajar. I'll write often. I'll wait for you to tell me the clouds aren't painted. And then I'll disagree. I'll tell you there are many things that we create that don't exist and never will. Like love. You'll say you prefer to deal in concrete.

ii

Downstairs, yesterday's chip wrappers are still splayed out on the kitchen table, housing half-eaten chips we couldn't finish. Even cold I can't resist the smell. I'll think of you. In the morning I'll wake with wings, newly pressed and fresh with wax. You'll doubt them wholly. I'll use them to seal our letters.

Afterwards

we find space
for whiskey-stained ghosts
to pass between our lips.

Tonight we'll mark
day's shortness with our breaths
and taught skins. Touching,

clouds of whispers dissipate
slow, linger cold—orbs hung low.

From the pavement,
streetlamps pick out laughter with
precision, watch it dance

with night 'til we fold
mesmerised by our own noises.
Tonight we are caught

moving just out of reach.
The cold never felt so warm.

Renaming

Come the morning he renames her in a coffee shop.
There is no ceremony in the half-drunk cappuccinos
or the teaspoon's sun-clad wink. The newspaper lies
spread-eagled on the table conspicuously unread.
Outside, May's bare sun tells her how to show calves
and knees in ways he swears he's never seen before.

Behind their sunglasses, eyes cannot make contact
so she studies his lips as they move, wants to know
how they work to form new sentences, new contracts
new names for all the old things. She sings it all back
to him, revels in the newness of her name caught
like teenagers in a kiss, learns how easy it is to be lost.

A poem in which the sky is a dark envelope

we slip between, hungry to devour the stars
and the walk home is full of night-silence and weight
where all our conversations find ground.

And you know it's not the same. The pavement
feels much harder without the vodka lift. I'm still looking
for Orion, as if he knows the way home.

And I like the precision, the light small
as a pip and so near tangible. His belt could be clung to
for days. And I'm an expert at navigation.

The first time we went to bed

you wondered at my deconstruction and its precision.
I was careful, you see. I wanted to melt slow as tears
welling under my skin. I wanted to be perfect

complete, didn't want to be the holes you'd fall through
later. I wanted to know I couldn't ruin it, wanted to
pretend I had nothing to hold back. I wanted to act

like it was nothing—knew wholly it was everything.

A poem in which we haven't talked about it yet

because I cannot give it proper names

because my lips won't form around certain words
and you'd hate to see me floundering

because when you approach it, the stab of it
is already there in the flinch of my stomach

because if we ignore it, we can pretend for a while

because I'd rather we didn't label my need
to control everything with it—I'd rather be quirky

because I don't yet know where I begin
and it ends and I don't care much for blurring

we haven't talked about it yet because
I don't know how to call it

Lines

I'd have written you a letter with my lips if I'd have been given
the chance, though the impermanence of it worries me greatly.

On the back of a postcard, I write to summon home. The smallness
of my hand allows more pain than I could have thought.

Despite my regiment, I loathe black lines and their formal endings.
I need a vastness the city cannot offer so I write with blue lines

to remind me of sky and sea. I write with damsons and desert ochres.
Even the note I write you to remind you to buy milk is written

twice. I worry about the paper I waste, keep it shelved, collected
in old shoe boxes. You long to throw them out when I'm not looking.

Search party

It's about this time
they'll tell me they sent the search party
                            and found nothing.

Fogged signals are red half-lights
glowing embers
                    in smoke-soft sky, framed charcoal.

Thick air fools me until I cannot resist the smell,
imagine charring and ash
in a hearth.
            Falling

I'm head over heels for the mundane
                    ceremonies we keep unknowingly

our playful stagger
of disappearances
                and rebirths.
                            Ancestry
                            is a broken thought.

        On this watch, I see every breath escape.

Dear boy

I want to tell you that I buried our bones in the garden last night
beneath the apple tree that barely fruits, even in her right season.
Without skin, I find it hard to contain myself. Please forgive me.
At times I can't help but cry for the limbs I no longer feel or want.
I like the way their shadows lie languid in the grass defying sun.
If I were a stone, I think I'd be happy though I'd mourn for the light
I absorb, wish for a star once in a while just to know how it felt
to be full of cold and brilliance. Please, tell me that you know
the voice of my feet as they shuffle on the kitchen lino, the sound
of my thoughts rushing through night as if they have places to be.
Tell me that you know what my name means to me, why it matters.
It's grave but I need to know how you can coil yourself so carefully
around my waist, how you taste my skin, kiss my salt-clad lips
how you find the curve drawn in my hips, when I refuse to exist.

Post-natal

You showed us how to measure time properly, how it falls
in the rise of your ribcage, makes space between your breaths.

Forget the years. This is about days, your age in minutes
countable on tiny digits and eyelashes in continuous tallies

a winter bird with a lonely first song. You show us how
to grab the light with your fist and hold it, your grasp of day

so much better than ours. But you weren't made to keep count
in the ways we did. When time fell short we wanted more.

At night your hair was a thousand earth-winged moths
twitching for the sun. That should have been my first clue.

Alley

I still hear
          the split of your laugh

the sound of the half-way dead, alive
        in the smallness
growing, dizzy on dark
               at the back of the old cinema

making homes for strays
and legends
          myths
          unravelling at the hems

our laces brambled tangles
and pockets
          bleeding an unpieced puzzle
on forgotten tarmac
discarded
          debris of our ghosts
turning walls in the day-lit hours
            until our echoes ring faint

and no-one remembers
          us
    or the traces that we left.

Before the birds begin

It'll be a while before the birds begin so please don't hold your breath.
I have watched you closely, and you I, both perplexed at why we speak
       nothing
of the storm that comes to rip our threads apart and shake our
       doll-faced selves
until our eyes rattle in their sockets, lolling stunned at what the world
       looks like
in jumped-up double-time.

Dark pupils take their time to recalculate, adjust, remember what it's like
to find each of our vertebrae sung free, skins colliding in their flights,
       longing
to dance the night from her stronghold, feel the pleasures of blistered
       soles
and silk's sweet friction burning above our knees, knowing the sun
       comes up
regardless of season and tidal shift.

Still, we know it'll be a while before the birds begin and we are restless
       with cold
and tired of keeping watch for fissured smiles and menacing, looking to
       ourselves
for porcelain and the ways she finely cracks.

Nightly

She longs to slip beneath the cloak of it, knows
it's only walls that keep us separate and blind.
The moon insists on making a ghost to dance

in panes, to sing just like she used to—silently,
in competition with the gulls. She cannot stand
the echoes, their hollowing of night, the piercing

repetition. It's the tiny backward glances that
hurt most. She makes them ink, hopes for quills
and cursive script, lines that cannot disappoint.

She leaves white sheets to be ruffled with crests.
Downstairs she abandons her lipstick 'til it swims
an oil slick on black tea, makes fish scale eyes

and swoons the curdling seas with their marble
so that nothing dares to stir, not even the birds
caught in the half-mooned dark between days.

On leaving me for the American

I was grateful you left me the sky, a glass of water on the side
a meniscus deep enough for air. I thought about drinking water
'til my bones grew soft, thought about being light enough

to sleep in the curve, to balance between wet and dry without
it feeling perilous. I thought without you I might be empty
hold a chasm like a lake so vast she keeps her own tide.

Water

I have no grave to lay cut flowers on so I think of it as sea ebbing
in the quiet of small morning hours, fresh dew left swelling in the light.

I think about the way our breaths condensed on our first window panes
the slow trickle of their downward path, the closeness of warmth.

In Spring's low sun I think about how I can measure the salt in my tears
imagine their dissolve, evaporation, the flat parch of the salt-pans.

When I touch fresh water I think of your skin, how it felt the first time
I put my finger in your palm and watched your fingers flex. I wonder

about your bones fragmented in the silt and if they keep the pace; if you
prefer her babbling or my constant silent prayers. In the presence

of water I'm a danger to myself, can't resist immersion, long to feel her
in my lungs despite her mortality. I try settling for cupping instead

hold her to my lips, breathe in before we kiss. It could never be enough.
In my kitchen I let the taps run, keep listening out for your voice.

Love begins in winter

In days of hard ground I am at my most solid, so show
me Spring through tiny frames. I'll need this weight
beneath my feet for balance, get caught blind in sun
of small proportions. I've grown so used to grey, her
squalid use of light. In these long hours when the sky
is blank having lost her stars, I am lost without her.
I need those holes, her clever lines and pin-taught light
the connections between to navigate by. Tomorrow
show me one small glimpse of blue and how it might fit.
Later lend me melancholy, know I'll borrow it gladly.

A conversation with the sun

is fruitless but I used to do it anyway
just in case it could make a difference.
I could never tell if she was listening
or holding her same blank stare.

Some days I wonder if the sky feels
the same holding her weight, never heard
mere canvas. I'd wanted to hear my voice
sound hollow and vast but in the end

it felt quite small and all I could think
about was how I could fit it in your
pocket, how you'd carry it unknowingly.
As she waned I knew she'd never be

the one. I needed something more
constant and certain, like flesh and lips
and a kiss like a moth pressing glass
in desperate search of the moon.

Air bubble

Imagine at first it's gentle, a squeezing of walls pushing in;
all about flex and resistance, a tightening 'til tension is obvious.
It's not a question of pain, it's much more complex than that.
In the end release is a pin-sized hole expanding exponentially
and we have no way to control it. When the air-lock folds
there is nothing, just air that needs to find new spaces to kiss,
to grasp. We want to hold it but wouldn't recognise its touch.

If we could believe this was all about numbers it would help.
Someone said quantity and regulation could be key. I tell them
consequence is not something to be quantified, that desert drag
makes us heated and fraught, friction-burnt, blind. The voice
of grief is deafening for those afflicted. There are no numbers
no codes for the longing of skin and hair, no scale to measure
the ways we wonder or the depth and volume of our cries.

Exile

In the year of writing sorrys
I wrote mine on postcards
from the concrete in my best
blue pen. I thought of you
by the sea, all that salt working
silently at healing and the sand
not helping at all. I waited
too long for your reply.

Another twenty, another stone

Here sheep are counted the old fashioned way; four pips,
another twenty, another stone. Gathered in my pocket
their sound is a heavy lullaby we wade knee deep in.
Their weight has a downdraught like a pin. The wind
collecting in my ears is sea flooding in, determined.
Tidal shifts are all that keep us balanced, the swing
a comfort we think we've had before but cannot place.
The edge is immeasurably distant from here, no matter
how much we stretch. The sky unfolds herself and lets in
light, grows vast as thought itself and we remain consumed.
Silt lies still 'til the ground falls flat now we realise how
wrong we've been standing. We've not learnt our lines
or their direction. Another twenty, another stone
waits pocketed, yearning to feel the ground.

Dungeness

You tell me there's so much more to it than this; neon
buoys and rope tongue-tied, the green and purple bruising
of the stones, flaked white paint and dull earth rust,
the stark division of the telegraph poles, birds lined up
neatly to watch. It could be much simpler than you think;
blue versus yellow, occasional rust. Instead you pick
the glass and rope, look for lost things in pallid sun
'til your chest puffs disappointed every time and I can't
understand it. It's all here in sagging metal, forgotten boats
like skeletons, all the things we find having lost their context,
placed strangely in squalid still lives, salt-clad silence
picking at the remnants, burning. The line between sky
and shingle could be iron, but it chooses to be thread.

Rooks

She takes her turn and waits. The rooks are a clockwork
mechanism made for gathering bones and this landing strip is littered.
You'd spat them out with mustard vigour, mouth running dry as hay
having no use for them now, you'd left them to grow old alone

heavy with the things we never said. Sometimes air gets held
tight as twigs in a blackbird's grip but it cannot make a nest, you said.
I didn't buy it until the machines came in to split the sums, make wounds
divide up land in a virus of furrows and crossed lines, watching

light breaking up with the dark.

Winter

I wanted to be knocked off-balance to feel the tide
in my stomach, turning; the white foam and salt,

the grit of it. I wanted the dark and the light, wanted
the sun flexing on the horizon and her shadows,

the contrast hard as pavement and clipped birds' calls.
I needed the sting of commuter hours,

to be reminded how it feels to bury my knees in sand,
leave my tongue in the moon, growing cold.

You laughed when my hands bruised. I drank the fog
and pretended it was sea.

Dead cert

You desire technicality. Time is a broken clock you dismantle
precisely only to stuff my cracking skin. I pretend I can make
it work. This time I'll try to remember what you taught me
when I was small; how snapping like a twig can be easy if you
let it happen, how to be above you without breaking a thing.
But there's an air of certainty about it; the way you split hairs
and bone, make small piles of me to store and count up later.

Even with my eyes closed I can watch the way you peel back
my skin like an offering, line your pockets with my ash. I feel
your rifle constantly. I work on letting myself go, like a swallow
hunting shores. I'm damn good at make-believe: it lets me slip
from you, uncovered. When I wake to white lights and echoes
I'll know this is not the heaven I'd bargained for and feel foolish
for my acceptance, for thinking lying still would hurt me less.

Long rock

You tell me it's the clarity of winter sun stretching out so leisurely that makes us forget her puckering. It makes us blind to the ways she laid them down so violently, kicked up kelp and shred it 'til it left bones and heart and lungs, their roots and plastic trophies all tangled and baking hard. She leaves us tide-marks in memoriam.

The longing to sleep beneath these salted weeds, a charred lump of driftwood black as winter nights, becomes as strong as churned sand making soft my face, salt-wind burning making sure it's set. But I am adrift in every wrong sense, my feet bound to ground and restless, carrying too much air in my lungs and not enough in my hair.

Creaturely

Maybe you'll catch me thinking of all the colours
we don't have names for yet, that exist without us
nonetheless. By their reckoning, it's possible we
have it wrong. I want to wear their eyes, see how
the light falls differently for myself, decipher their
calls while they make the shape of their own names,
pretend to know. I wonder how we might make it up
exchange concrete for moor, find night has colour
we couldn't have known, wonder what they'd make
of heather. It's a shame, there's no way of knowing
how their palette shifts between the neon lights
and empty skies, what shades they make from sea,
whether they know the cold of September's steel,
the burning of umbers all throughout November.

Departing

I bring home flowers and roll the petals on
my tongue, wait for stones to form then spit.

I watch them play the light, count them slipping
through my fingers. Boxed, I save it all for later

dip bare skin in scented wax and touch the moon.
Outside wolves make pacts, sleep showing teeth

while I draw back my eyes with kohl, plait hair.
I drink you in tots of nectar stuck to glass, scent

enough to slice the air like bog. Every time
the wick gets lit, I watch it burn and sing.

Icon

Inside the table was a 40s icon
chairs gathered 'round, tucked in
like   house-trained   children
brought   up   the   strict way.
You   were   my   grandmother's
damson   jam,   ink   on   the   jar
a little cross I'd always mistaken
for a kiss, a spoon's knowing
wink to a bare ceiling light
on the side, on the tile we'd used
for   a   coaster,   hand-painted
flowers   curling   on   the   wood.
Afterwards   the   radio   refused
to   sing   the   way   it   used   to
the sun rising silent in the glass
so   as   not   to   be   noticed
slipping   in   days   right   under
our   noses.   It   seems   strange
what   we   do   not   miss.

Penny whistle

In the night I dream you are an orchestra of penny whistles
house martin chatter, gentle cawing of sea birds calling days
to their close. I map swift flight precisely, trust it knows its path.

I long for you to tell me how you still sing despite us, that you
still have things you want to say, that in the storm of our unending
noise you wish and long for louder lungs. We are all drowned

in the concrete sometimes, ears strained and searching for
your penny whistle songs. I swell with disappointment when I
cannot tune in, miss your well-strung notes and grieve.

Sound

Even at first it was the ghost of you
a white crooked crescent blurring in the move
you struggled even then to know what light was for
camera-shy and shuffling back to nothing but feeling
speaking languages just for me.

Only you and I know what it's like
to hold a thousand tiny heartbeats right here
in the pits of us, how they talk and laugh and dance
softly with reminders, as if we ever needed them
of how we thought this might be.

Girl in the dog-tooth coat

The last of you was seen wandering the hills
a few weeks later, your red hair loose and wild

flung in every direction. I thought you might
be looking for sky. I didn't tell on you though,

don't worry, I kept your secrets sewn inside
my ribs for safe keeping. Now when I walk

through slate and bog cotton I know my feet
have found your footprints, that in breathing

this wind, the song of you is almost audible.

On not holding on to a bird

Let me tell you how hard I've worked to grow you, how much time.
I feel you ready to burst these skins and still you refuse to come; feel
the sting of your stunting, the anticipation of your release. I want you
to let me teach you how to be nomadic, how to make the best of it,
how to nest, how to move on when time is right. I want you to drop
your anchor, then leave it behind; to feel the wind and the blue of sky,
the power of cold carbon clouds, the surge of energy through thunder.
Let me talk to you in coded tones until you begin to know what there is
to decipher. I'm not pretty but a siren, a signpost to navigate home by.
Let me share with you those magpies who only ever sing the blues;
just look at how they dress, their suits and spats, black against white.
Know it's a mistake to think of them as constant sad. Let me tell you
how flight lets you forget the origins of your thoughts, your shape;
how the sky works hard to teach you all the ways that you might sing.

Sticks

In the sticks the rails are silences in small hours
cease to be at midnight, do not wake 'til five.

Beneath your eyelash stitching I wonder if the lights
still echo in your iris, stunning as a permafrost

in the dark. I know you feel the ache, in the place
behind your temples where you keep our face framed

with the gilding of a whiskey glow, the band making
something from the corner while I watch you dance

through the door. Tonight there'll be no flinch
in the sticks, even when the crows laugh prematurely

into the glass and the sky is a highly punctuated letter
of discontent stirring, dragging the world awake.

Sleep for the insomniac

You'll not find me in the dark, still dream of me open-eyed
drenched in camomile, stewing. I am not there in the stench
but in the spring that's breaking behind the horizon. Long for
clarity like mint from your mother's garden with it's soft sweet
sting and the pitch of her chlorophyll steep. Long for meadow,
long for the beach. Know that I am not in the place you think
about constantly. I am not a cave to be lost in. I am the sun
on your back, gentle and warm. I am the grass and the earth,
patchworked sky, new air. I am water to float on, not to sink.

Oblate spheroid

There are times that I get sick from the small discrepancies
in our computations. I have the restlessness my Mother had
in my blood. You give me mechanics and I long for a sense
of it. Instead I get gold weight, celestial charts, calibration.
In rotation we become elliptical. I lose my faith in geometry,
its rigidity. Off-kilter we are a constant slur and I fall often
'til scabs form on my knee. All I can think about is the moon,
the surface I spent cold nights longing for in full, red eclipse.
I've tried learning how it feels to look down. Transcendence
reminds me of birds in formation over sea, using the current
for rise and fall. I think about that soft salt kiss. Every time
my last breath falls out in one slow sigh, a trail of white silk
suspended in air so we might get its measure. I draw it back
in eventually. The dissipation makes it easier to swallow.

Something for nothing

For a while, let me be blank as the city
in the pre-dawn, listening for birds before
they stir, watching light and its gradual
slipping. I want to be sure that this is no
time, nothing to be measured in numbers
or complicated factorials, to know that
it's felt, fabric on skin, breath in lungs
chimes in our chests. Know that it's ok
to abandon me here, a bench on the south
side of the Thames as it begins to realise
it's alive again, that I'll be anything and
nothing, maybe even something. I'll sing
and be silent all at once.

Echoes

It's the constant punctuation of our thoughts   despite our efforts
at tuning out. I want to hear your chest rise   and the clock tick
but I find myself drifting to a place of no machinery at all   and I
can't quite grasp it. These blank corridors echo and   I am easy
to disorientate. Every metaphor about space   and floating has
since been spent and I am left with nylon   static, scratching skin.
And yes, I know you are the blanket I recycle   time after time.
When they switched the machines off I swear   you nearly breathed.

On being lost

Not against the loss itself but the phrasing
that makes me careless, you misplaced

and the words that make it seem as if you
might be found one day, might yet return

might yet appear between the grass guided
home by the petrolled wings of magpies

forked tails of martins, sea sounds echoing
through these four walls and windows

that I might yet feel foolish for knowing
that wherever you are lost, I am too

that the ashes we gave the ground mean
nothing, nothing concrete at all.

Numbers

Afterwards they asked me for numbers.
I felt neglectful; I'd never kept count.
Estimating is pure mechanics and I was
sparing with my digits. Still balancing
the equations never seemed quite right.
What did it matter anyway, when once
is enough for everyone? Ten, twenty,
fifty, eighty—written down, it's qualified
measured in cold key taps, bare fact.
I gave them all my numbers knowing
they mean nothing. They mistook them
for answers. I knew they would.

Acknowledgements

Thanks are due to the editors of the following print and online literary magazines, in which some of the poems first appeared: *Popshot, The Interpreters House, Ink, Sweat & Tears, HARK, Lampeter Review, Obsessed with Pipework, Belleville Park Pages, Lantern, Yellow Chair Review, Euonia Review, Prole, Nutshells and Nuggets, Dog Ear, Bare Fiction Magazine, Lunar Poetry.*

'Another twenty, another stone' was the winner of the Battered Moons Poetry Competition 2014.

'Creaturely' was Commended in the Café Writers Open Poetry Competition 2014.

Special thanks must be said to: Robert Harper for his editorial guidance, patience and support. Jo Bell, Catherine Ayres, Hannah Linden, Joanne Key, Mary Gilonne, Beth McDonough, the entire 52 project, Helen Ivory, Angela Readman, George Szirtes, Harry Man, Rosie Sherwood, Jacob Denno, Nick Murray, Freya Morris, Sam Loveless, Richard Skinner, Ian Chung, Tam Purkess, Stephen Daniels. Jayne Anita Smith for her wonderful cover illustration. Jim Stapley, for believing. My dear and patient family and friends.